COMMEMORATIVE POTTERY & PORCELAIN

The 18th and 19th centuries celebrated their heroes and victories, their public and private occasions, not only in song, but also with inscribed and decorated mugs and plates and jugs and punchbowls. Today the rarer pieces are costly antiques.

Many of them, however, can be picked up for a song, and these heirlooms of the future are easily acquired, for there has been a great revival of interest in commemorative pottery in recent years. Pictorial rack-plates have been made to mark the first moon landing; pottery mugs in honour of Prince Charles's Investiture; Christmas plates, Mayflower plates, plaques commemorating the bicentenary of Captain Cook's voyage to the Pacific, a plate marking the golden jubilee of the Royal Air Force, jasperware to celebrate that of the Girl Guides . . . the list is long and fascinating.

This is the *first book* on this subject, and is a stimulating and beautifully illustrated introduction to evocative objects which could find their way into any household, written by a collector of them.

These books by James Mackay are also published by
Garnstone Press, London

AN INTRODUCTION TO SMALL ANTIQUES
COIN COLLECTING FOR GROWN-UP BEGINNERS

Coming
STAMP COLLECTING FOR GROWN-UP BEGINNERS

This book is published by Garnstone Press, London,
who issue a wide range of attractive non-fiction titles in
the fields of communications, history, philosophy, hobbies,
literature, London information and travel. Their catalogue is
always available free on request.

COMMEMORATIVE POTTERY & PORCELAIN

James Mackay

Garnstone Press

COMMEMORATIVE POTTERY & PORCELAIN
is published by
Garnstone Press Limited
59 Brompton Road, London sw3

ISBN 0 900391 68 5

Printed by *A Wheaton & Company, Exeter*

Contents

Illustrations

The author and publishers are grateful to the following for providing photographs; Christie, Manson & Woods for Plates 2, 4, 5, 9, 10, 13, 14, 16; Sotheby & Co for Plates 1, 6, 7, 8; the Wedgwood Group for Plates 3, 12, 15, 18, 19, 20, 21, 22, 23, 24, 25; Minton Ltd for Plate 11; Phillips, Son & Neale for Plates 26, 27, and Spode-Copeland for Plate 17.

Foreword

Over the past four centuries decorative pottery has been produced to commemorate some person or event. The origins of this branch of ceramics may be traced back to the faenza and maiolica of Italy and Western Europe in the late Renaissance period, but undoubtedly the greatest flowering of what was essentially a folk art came in the eighteenth and early nineteenth centuries, particularly in England where the Staffordshire potters were quick to record contemporary affairs and personalities in this manner.

From the collector's viewpoint there has been a marked revival of interest in commemorative pottery in recent years. Significantly also, a fair amount of that more precious substance, porcelain, is now being devoted to commemorative wares. The fashion for commemorative rack-plates has made a dramatic come-back, while the Investiture of the Prince of Wales at Caernarvon Castle in 1969 greatly stimulated interest in pottery and porcelain connected with royal events in general.

There is, as yet, no handbook devoted to this fascinating aspect of ceramics, although both general and specialised works occasionally touch on the subject. This short book is offered simply as an introduction to this facet of ceramics and an indication of the enormous scope which it offers, both for pleasure and, as I note from steeply rising prices, profit.

In the compilation of this book I am indebted to the public relations officers of Copeland-Spode, Josiah Wedgwood, Minton, Royal Doulton and Royal Worcester, not only for information on their wares, but for many of the illustrations. In addition, pictures of antique items of commemorative pottery and porcelain have been supplied by Christie, Manson & Woods, Phillips, Son & Neale and Sotheby & Co.

James Mackay

An Orsini-Colonna jar.
Early sixteenth century
Italian faenza ware.

The earliest examples of pottery in which the decoration incorporates a commemorative device or motif are the tin-glazed earthenwares popular from the Italian Renaissance to the early years of the eighteenth century. Tin-enamel glazes on pottery are of immense antiquity; they have been found on pottery dating from the tenth century B.C. in Mesopotamia and, after a long period in oblivion, were revived by Persian craftsmen at the time of the Mohammedan invasions of the eighth century A.D. The spread of Islam across North Africa and into southern Spain brought this distinctive type of earthenware to Europe. Generally known as Hispano-Mauresque ware, this brightly decorated pottery spread to France via the island of Majorca and from this was derived the word maiolica, by which the Italian tin-glazed earthenware of the fifteenth and sixteenth centuries is often known. Other names for the same thing are faience or faenza (after the Italian town of Faenza, which was a notable centre of production) and delft (from the Dutch town whence this earthenware spread throughout the Low Countries, Germany and Britain).

The brilliant enamel colours used by craftsmen to decorate their wares were developed at a time when the art of painting in Renaissance Italy was undergoing tremendous expansion. In the early sixteenth century painting superseded sculpture in popularity and it was not long before artists were applying the new techniques of the canvas to tin-enamel glaze. The result was the lavishly decorated plates, jugs, jars and dishes which characterised Italian maiolica. Particularly popular were the *istoriato* or history-painting techniques. Examples of *istoriato* decoration drew on mythology and the Bible for inspiration, but many cases are known in which events and personalities, either contemporary or of the recent past, were depicted.

An excellent example in this *genre* is the faenza double-handled jar, formerly in the Di Tella Collection, bearing the portrait of a man wearing a green and blue hat. This jar, used as a container for drugs, was one of a long series of so-called Orsini-Colonna jars, made to celebrate the cessation of hostilities between the two families. Many of the persons depicted on the early Italian drug jars, or *Albarelli* as they are known,

William of Orange portrait charger. English delftware c 1690.

are unidentified. More readily recognisable, however, are the beautiful dishes which were a speciality of the town of Urbino. Scenes from Roman history were a prime favourite: portraits of such heroes of the early Roman kingdom as Manius Curtius or Mucius Scaevola, scenes from the Punic Wars or the lives of the Emperors. Others drew on Biblical incidents: Joseph sold into captivity, the Judgment of Solomon, Moses and the Ten Commandments are typical examples from the Old Testament, while the Nativity, the Crucifixion and scenes from the life of Our Lord provided material from the New Testament. The exploits of St Paul and the lives of the saints were also a fertile field.

To a lesser extent Biblical scenes furnished subjects for the Dutch and English artists who decorated delftware plates and chargers in the late sixteenth and early seventeenth centuries. Two Dutchmen, Janson and Andries, established a pottery at Lambeth in 1570 and built up a flourishing business for the manufacture of pots, jugs and jars. Significantly the earliest dated example of English delftware is a large plate, or charger, of 1600 showing a view of the Tower of London. In the ensuing decades chargers produced for purely ornamental purposes became very popular. These vigorously decorated pieces were the forerunners of the rack-plates of the eighteenth and nineteenth centuries which have enjoyed an astonishing revival in recent years.

The turbulent events in Britain and Ireland at the end of the seventeenth century inspired numerous delftware chargers of a political nature. The best known of these depicted a royal equestrian figure, the identity of the monarch being deliberately left unspecified. It may be that the potter left it to his clients to see in the portrait either James II or William of Orange, according to their loyalties!

13

The Industrial Revolution in England, which coincided with the accession of King George III in 1760, touched off a wave of popular prosperity equalled in no other country either before or since. The movement from the land to the new towns and cities, the rapid industrialisation which reached its peak about 1850, the enormous colonial expansion of this period and the mushroom growth of the population, resulted in tremendous social and economic upheavals. Not the least of these was the emergence of a working class which not only had money to spend, but often a surplus of cash. In those days before the spread of popular saving, many people lived from day to day and spent their money as fast as it came. This was the market to which the Staffordshire potters catered during the latter half of the eighteenth and the first half of the nineteenth centuries.

For the first time in history the lower income groups began to adorn their homes—if not in the manner of the aristocracy and the upper classes, at least in a modest style which was consciously or unconsciously influenced by them. If the working classes could not afford Meissen or Sèvres, Chelsea or Derby porcelain, at least they could purchase cheap earthenware 'toys' manufactured by the Staffordshire potters and hawked from door to door by chapmen and pedlars.

At one end of the scale large commercial organisations such as Minton or Wedgwood produced good earthenware, salt-glazed stoneware, basaltes or terracotta figures, characters from history and mythology or even contemporary celebrities, such as Voltaire or the American Benjamin Franklin. The vast bulk of the industry, however, was in the hands of the tiny potbanks, often consisting of a single potter and his family, in which even the young children took a hand in the modelling and decoration. The majority of the pieces produced by this cottage industry were unmarked, so we know comparatively little about the families and small businesses who made these intriguing figures. Certain potters, such as John Astbury and Thomas Whieldon, however, have long been household names to collectors of eighteenth-century folk art and the figures which they and others like them produced are now in great demand.

The subjects ranged from royalty (George II and George III) to popular heroes such as Clive of India and Dolly Pentreath, the Welshwoman who tricked the French invaders of Pembrokeshire into surrender in 1798. One of the most famous of all the contemporary subjects which captured the imagination of the potters and their customers at the end of the eighteenth century was the French Revolution; the assassination of Marat by Charlotte Corday was the subject of a finely modelled figure group by Lakin & Poole of Burslem. Popular figures, preachers like John Wesley, social workers and philanthropists such as Hannah Moore and William Wilberforce, were immortalised in figures and busts in a wide variety of materials from enamelled earthenware to pearlware and stoneware. Even popular enemies like Napoleon Bonaparte came in for treatment at the hands of the Staffordshire potters and it is interesting to compare the naive qualities of an enamelled earthenware bust of Napoleon with the sensitivity of the black basalte busts which Wedgwood popularised.

Apart from figures and busts many of the commemorative pieces produced in Staffordshire and the surrounding region were utilitarian, bowls, jugs and mugs being the vessels most favoured. An unusual pottery jug sold at Christie's in 1968 had its sides decorated with scenes captioned 'Marquis Wellington in the Field of Battle' and 'The Narrow Escape of Boney through a Window'.

The fashion for commemorative pottery established by the Staffordshire potters, and continued down to the present day in the products of Wedgwood, seldom attracted the attentions of the porcelain manufacturers, although there were occasions throughout the nineteenth century when commemorative pieces were produced in this much more expensive medium. The best known examples are the literary figures produced by Derby; a fine figure of Milton standing in pensive mood beside a pedestal moulded in relief with the Expulsion from Paradise is recorded from this factory in the eighteenth century, but the more plentiful figures were those produced in the Bloor Derby period, based on the statues modelled by Scheemakers for Westminster Abbey.

Occasionally nineteenth-century porcelain bowls and jugs are found with a commemorative inscription added to the decoration, as, for example, the Mansfield jug sold at Sotheby's in December 1969. The landscape and floral decoration, probably by Billingsley, included an inscription honouring 'Lieut. General John Barclay, General Commandant Royal Marines'.

Doulton's of Lambeth, better known in the nineteenth

A modern Wedgwood medallion of John Keats.

century for their sanitary wares, produced a number of commemorative mugs, mainly in connection with royal events (and therefore discussed later in greater detail), but in addition produced stoneware jugs from 1884 onwards in memory of General Gordon. The earliest of these had a buff ovoid body with a green medallion portrait of the General flanked by quotations from his writings: 'By the help of God I will hold the balance level' and 'I decline to agree that your expedition is for me'—statements which, after this passage of time, seem rather obscure, but no doubt intrigue the collector into delving into the curious political background to Gordon's exploits in the Sudan.

The origin of the name Toby in this connection is obscure, though most authorities now attribute it to the poem, published in 1761, about the hearty toper Toby Fillpot. The last verse of this poem by the Reverend Francis Hawkes ran:

> His body, when long in the Ground it had lain
> And time into Clay had resolv'd it again
> A potter found out in its Covert so snug
> And with part of fat Toby he form'd this brown jug.

This poem inspired an engraving of Toby Fillpot published by Carington Bowles after a design by Robert Dighton. This in turn inspired Ralph Wood of Burslem to manufacture jugs in Toby's image from about 1765 onwards. Other potters were not long in emulating the Ralph Wood jugs and eventually there was a wide range of them, from the simple Toby, the Thin Man, the Snuff-taker, the Sailor and the Parson to those whose origins can be traced to actual personages and which are therefore, in a sense, commemorative pottery.

In the latter category come the female Toby jugs commemorating Martha Gunn, the well-known bathing attendant at Brighton; she is sometimes depicted with the three feather emblem of the Prince of Wales, an allusion to her royal patronage. The Bluff King Hal Toby is said to represent the Prince Regent (later King George IV) who wore the costume of King Henry VIII at a Brighton masquerade. The closest that the Staffordshire potters of the eighteenth and early nineteenth centuries ever came to portraying a national hero in this manner was the Lord Howe Toby. This jug, modelled by Ralph Wood, showed the redoubtable admiral seated on a barrel with a pipe at the side and a dog at his feet. He is usually shown in black tricorn hat and naval coat and pale yellow breeches.

Toby jugs have continued to appear right down to the present time. Late nineteenth-century examples featured Gladstone and Disraeli. During the First World War F. Carruthers Gould modelled a series of eleven famous personages on the Allied side and these consisted of King George V seated on his throne and holding a globe, President Wilson

Toby jugs in the form of Lord Howe and Admiral Rodney. Late eighteenth century.

with an aeroplane, the base inscribed 'Welcome Uncle Sam', Marshal Joffre with a shell inscribed in dreadful punning French '*Ce que j'offre*' (that which I offer), Admiral Beatty with a shell inscribed 'Dread Naught', Lloyd George, his shell inscribed 'Shell out', General Sir John French with a jug inscribed '*French pour les Francais*', Marshal Foch with a bottle inscribed '*Au Diable le Kaiser*', Field Marshal Haig sitting on a tank inscribed 'Push and go', Kitchener with a jug inscribed 'Bitter for the Kaiser', Admiral Jellicoe inscribed 'Hell Fire Jack', General Botha with a jug inscribed 'Loyalty' and Winston Churchill (then First Lord of the Admiralty) holding a battleship, with the inscription 'May God defend the right'. Incidentally, the late Sir Winston Churchill was the subject of innumerable wartime Toby jugs of the Second World War and Royal Doulton have a Winston Churchill Toby still in current production.

Analagous to the Toby jugs are the Character jugs which originated in Staffordshire in the middle of the eighteenth century. Curiously enough, although mugs in the shape of faces were widely produced from that time onward, the only one which can definitely be identified as a specific person is that featuring Admiral Lord Rodney. Rodney mugs were popular in the 1790s and are found in pearlware, stoneware and Leeds creamware, as well as coloured Staffordshire earthenware. A modern counterpart of the Rodney mugs are the Churchill mugs manufactured in recent years. Again, no other famous person seems to have been accorded this curious tribute.

Since 1960 Royal Doulton have produced a lengthy series of Character jugs, many of which feature characters associated with colonial Williamsburg in the United States. The majority of the Doulton jugs, however, are based on literary figures or people in folklore, such as Merlin and Robin Hood. The only jugs based on actual historical personages are those devoted to Captain Sir Henry Morgan, the famous buccaneer turned colonial governor, and Dick Turpin the notorious highway-man.

4 Victorian Flat-backs

Probably the best known of all the Staffordshire figures are the flat-backs of the middle and late Victorian period. These hollow moulded pieces, with their simple oval bases and distinctive flat backs, suddenly became very popular in the 1840s, having evolved out of the flower vases and spill-holders made from the end of the eighteenth century onward. Public demand for simple ornaments to decorate the chimney-pieces of mid-Victorian cottages, combined with attempts on the part of the manufacturers to streamline production techniques and thus cut costs, led to the appearance of the flat-back figure groups.

Kilted highlanders, wide-eyed milkmaids and naive spaniels formed the bulk of the figures throughout the latter half of the nineteenth century, when the vogue for chimney ornaments was at its peak.

The marriage of Queen Victoria and Prince Albert in 1840, however, also inspired the production of pottery portrait figures of famous people and these, on account of their allusions, are now eagerly sought after. Figures of the Queen and the Prince Consort were turned out in thousands to satisfy patriotic sentiment. In due course they were followed by similar figures inscribed 'Prince and Princess' featuring the young Prince of Wales and his sister Princess Victoria Louise. The success of these groups induced the Staffordshire potters to extend the range of royal figures. The dowager Queen Adelaide (who died in 1849) was the subject of flat-back groups while foreign royalty, such as Tsar Alexander I of Russia, Kaiser Franz II of Austria and the Empress Eugenie of France, were also immortalised in these robust pottery figures. The perennial favourites, however, were the British Royal Family. The numerous progeny of Queen Victoria, from infancy to middle age, provided the potters with a never-ending source of material for which there was always a ready sale.

Many celebrities of a more ephemeral nature were also portrayed in this manner, and in this category come popular heroes and politicians, prize-fighters and lion-tamers. Religious subjects form an important group, ranging from Biblical

Victorian flat-back figures.
Staffordshire c 1860.

characters to the exploits of popular saints and the martyrdom of Latimer and Ridley. The latter, though commemorating events of three centuries earlier, were given a topical twist by the Papal Bull of 1850 giving territorial rights to Catholic bishops in Britain. Contemporary religious figures from John Wesley to the American revivalists Moody and Sankey were reproduced in pottery.

Almost as popular were figures connected with crime. Highwaymen turned folk heroes, such as Dick Turpin and his accomplice Tom King, are comparatively plentiful, but much scarcer and in greater demand are the figures of James Rushton and Emily Sandford, connected with the notorious Stanfield Hall murder of 1849, or William Corder and his victim Maria Martin of the Polstead murder of 1828.

Geographical considerations and an adventurous character combined to make the British a maritime power unrivalled for centuries until within living memory. The greatest national heroes—from Drake to Rodney, from Nelson to Beatty—were seamen, and even the kings who were assured of the greatest popular following in their own generation and afterwards were those like Alfred the Great or Henry VIII who built the Navy or who, like William IV or George V, actually went to sea. It is hardly surprising, therefore, that an important category of commemorative pottery and porcelain is that which pertains to the sea—commemorating naval battles, honouring famous sailors or depicting famous ships.

Among the first of the popular heroes to receive ceramic honours was Admiral Edward Vernon, the fiery sea-dog turned politician who, in the House of Commons in 1739, denounced the conduct of the war then being fought with Spain in the West Indies. Vernon claimed that, given six ships only, he could capture the Spanish naval base at Portobello. The government took him at his word and fitted out an expedition under his command which actually *did* seize Portobello on 22 November 1739, with the loss of only seven men. Overnight Vernon became a national hero; public-houses were renamed in his honour, one of London's most famous roads was christened after the event, and popular souvenirs were churned out by the thousand for his adoring fans. Incidentally Admiral Vernon was nicknamed 'Old Grog' on account of his habit of wearing grogram trousers, and the beverage of rum diluted in water (which he introduced into the Royal Navy) is known as 'grog' in his memory to this day. Plates in Lambeth delft or Bristol blue-and-white ware were produced with his portrait or stirring action scenes of his ships in Portobello Harbour. These plates were near contemporary to the event and the person honoured, but Vernon and Portobello continued to be a favourite subject of the potters for several generations and mugs, bowls and jugs, in different materials and styles of treatment, were produced from 1740 until Queen Victoria's time.

The majority of the naval heroes honoured by British

potters were, naturally, Englishmen. A curious exception, however, was the intrepid Dutch admiral Van Tromp whom Ralph Wood immortalised in earthenware figures. Van Tromp got the better of his British adversaries on several occasions, but, like Rommel in the Second World War, earned the respect of his enemies. After the third Dutch war he even visited England, where he was well received by Charles II.

Britain had little to celebrate in the disastrous war of 1776–83 which resulted in the independence of the United States, but one of the great morale boosters of the period was Admiral Rodney's decisive defeat of the combined French and Spanish fleets in the Battle of the Saints in 1782. This victory inspired the well-known Staffordshire potter Enoch Wood to produce a circular plaque with the admiral's profile and the inscription 'Success to GB Rodney'. This slogan, or variants of it, appeared on mugs and earthenware tankards in the latter years of the eighteenth century. Comparatively scarce are plates and bowls adorned in similar fashion; a fine Liverpool bowl inscribed 'Success to the Brave Rodney' was sold at Christie's in 1967.

The heyday of British maritime power occurred during the Napoleonic Wars and the many naval engagements of this period provided the pottery manufacturers with numerous subjects for commemoration or adulation. A large collection could be formed with Lord Nelson as the theme. Items range from Wedgwood jasper medallions and basaltes busts to the homely flat-back figures of mid-Victorian times. In between these two extremes come the Prattware jugs portraying Nelson and his aide, Captain Hardy (an alternative figure is Captain Berry), and the stoneware jugs by Doulton and Watts. Derby produced a porcelain mug to commemorate the Battle of the Nile in 1798, while an unknown manufacturer was responsible for cups and saucers celebrating the Battle of Trafalgar. The decoration on these pieces is interesting. The saucer shows the English ships in line ahead, bearing down on the French in line ahead, with the coast of Cape Trafalgar outlined. A portrait of Nelson, after the picture by Lemuel Abbott in the National Maritime Museum, appeared on the cup.

Wedgwood jasper medallions, late eighteenth—early nineteenth century.
Left: Charles James Fox
Right: Lord Nelson

Nelson's illustrious contemporaries, such as Jarvis and St Vincent, Duncan and Howe, also received their share of honour in the pottery of the late eighteenth and early nineteenth centuries, but even relatively obscure figures were celebrated. A small Prattware jug is recorded with moulded relief portraits of Admiral Duncan and 'Captain Trolop' (*sic*), made to celebrate the victory at Camperdown. Captain Henry Trollope was subsequently knighted for his part in the action, while Duncan was created Viscount Duncan of Camperdown. A Staffordshire jug is known with a decoration of sailing ships and the inscriptions 'Success to the Shark' and

Prattware plaques of
Admiral Lord Howe (right)
and Admiral Duncan (left).
Late eighteenth century.

'Capt. Matthews Mr. 1804', while a creamware jug of 1794 has the legend 'Success to the Wilding'.

Nearer our own time the First World War inspired the Staffordshire mug inscribed 'God Save King George V' and 'Long Live the British Navy' with a portrait of Admiral David Beatty decorating the side.

At the present day the launching of the latest Cunarder, *Queen Elizabeth 2*, has been commemorated in plates and dishes produced by the Crown Staffordshire pottery, while Wedgwood's have recently issued an attractive Trafalgar mug, showing the British battle fleet and a portrait of Admiral Lord Nelson.

A finely decorated North-umbrian jug depicting the opening of the Liverpool and Manchester Railway in the 1830s.

In the field of communications Britain was notable in the eighteenth century for her mastery of the sea; in the following century she was equally noted for her development of internal transport by means of railways. No other country in the world, either then or since, had such a highly developed network of railways; indeed, it could be argued that Britain was over-developed in this respect and the 'rationalisation' of uneconomic lines is a slow and painful but inevitable process which is still in progress.

Just as the potters were quick to reflect national pride in maritime prowess with the sort of naval pottery discussed in the foregoing chapters, so also they were prolific producers of wares with a railway theme. The majority of the items thus decorated consisted of mugs, tankards and jugs; shaving mugs, plates, vases and bowls are less frequently met with, but every type of vessel and dish was subjected to this form of ornamentation and all are highly prized nowadays by railway enthusiasts.

The subjects ranged from pictures of the early locomotives to views of stations, viaducts, railway bridges and cuttings. The majority were probably produced to popularise the subject and were mainly pictorial in concept but the most highly desirable items were produced in connection with a specific occasion, perhaps the opening of a new line or the inauguration of a railway station. Most of the potteries, and even a few of the porcelain manufacturers, seem to have been attracted to this subject at some time or another. It is interesting to note that, by contrast, comparatively little interest was shown by the potters in coaching scenes. No doubt it was a case of familiarity breeding contempt, whereas the iron horse and the puffing billy had modernity and novelty to commend them.

Many important collections of ceramics have been devoted to this subject alone, those of John Phillimore and C. F. Dendy Marshall having been particularly famous in the period before the Second World War. The largest collection of railway pottery to come up at auction in recent years was that disposed of by Sotheby's in Toronto in October 1967.

One of the major centres for the manufacture of English delftware outside London was Bristol, and it seems that in that district the people took their politics very seriously indeed. A distinctive feature of the Bristol delftware was its preoccupation with contemporary political events, plates being produced bearing slogans in favour of various parliamentary candidates. Judging from the dated examples the period when these electioneering plates were in vogue was the 1750s. From the election for the Tewkesbury constituency in 1754, for example, come plates bearing such inscriptions as 'Sir Ino Pole for Ever, 1754' or 'Nugent only, 1754', while a third bears the names of two candidates—'Calvert and Martin for Tukesbury 1754'. It is important to remember that prior to the Parliamentary Reform of 1832 parliamentary boroughs in England and Wales returned two members each to the

House of Commons. Another plate dating from the same election bore the legend 'Fortescue & Harris For Ever, 1754'. An undated plate with a more than usually ornamented border was inscribed 'Cresswell Esqr For Ever'. It is likely that this plate is contemporary with the others since Cresswell is known to have been Member of Parliament for Wootton Bassett in 1757.

Although electioneering plates seem to have been extremely shortlived, politics continued to obtrude into commemorative wares at various times. One of the greatest *causes célèbres* in the middle of the eighteenth century was the affair of John Wilkes, Member of Parliament for Aylesbury, and editor of the *North Briton*, who was imprisoned in 1763 on a libel charge for attacking Lord Bute, the Tory Prime Minister. Although released from prison Wilkes was expelled from Parliament and

Chinese Famille Rose
punch bowl decorated with
the theme of John Wilkes
and Liberty. c 1765.

his various attempts to secure re-election as a Member for Middlesex were thwarted. Eventually he was allowed to take his seat in 1774 and in the same year became Lord Mayor of London. The turbulent 1760s made Wilkes the darling of the radical opposition and inspired a great deal of pottery and even porcelain inscribed 'Wilkes and Liberty' and bearing his portrait. Some interesting examples of this sort were displayed in the Wilkes Exhibition at the British Museum in 1968, including a rare creamware teapot in the possession of Viscount Eccles. Christie's sale of Chinese Export Porcelain in November 1969 included an interesting Famille Rose punch bowl enamelled *en grisaille* and gilt with the famous picture of Wilkes carrying a pole and the cap of Liberty.

Generally speaking, political events passed the pottery manufacturers by, but one notable exception was the New Marriage Act of 1822, the first of a long series of acts regularising the law on marriage. By this Act the minimum age for marriage without consent was fixed at 21 years and it was this aspect which was attacked or satirised by the Staffordshire potters. Earthenware figure groups showing a young couple's wedding ceremony are known with the caption 'John Frill and Ann Boke, aged 21; That is right says the Parson; Amen says the Clerk'. Several variants of this group are known with the same names.

Popular patriotics began to influence commemorative pottery only in comparatively recent times. From the time of the Boer War come plates and mugs decorated with the military heroes of the day, embellished with suitable slogans. Very much in demand by collectors today is a Copeland 'Transvaal War' loving cup, the sides transfer-printed with heroic motifs and patriotic inscriptions. This item was produced in a limited edition of 100 for Thomas Goode and Co. Royal Worcester produced a porcelain figure of a Tommy in khaki uniform at about the same time.

Patriotic plates from the First World War are relatively scarce, though one example noted recently bore the text of a speech by Lloyd George exhorting the 'home front' to redouble their efforts in support of the war.

Most people, collectors and laymen alike, would invariably associate commemorative pottery with Jubilee and Coronation mugs, for this class of ware, mass-produced in connection with the celebration of important royal events, constitutes the most popular and best-known of all commemorative ceramics.

It is surprising to note how ancient is the tradition of such celebratory pieces. Lambeth delftware plates are known inscribed 'God Save the King, 1660' in honour of the Restoration of King Charles II, while F. H. Garner, in his book *English Delftware* (1948) illustrated a Lambeth mug portraying Charles II and dated 1660. Such examples are of great rarity and the practice of producing mugs and plates in honour of royal events did not become general until the early nineteenth century. From the accession of King George IV in 1820 onwards mugs in porcelain and pottery of various kinds, decorated with portraits of kings and queens and other members of the Royal Family, became increasingly frequent, though the first occasion on which Coronation mugs were mass-produced for general distribution was in honour of King Edward VII in 1902. Since then there has been a plethora of Coronation souvenirs in pottery and porcelain, marking the Coronations of George V (1911), George VI (1937) and Queen Elizabeth (1953). Of great interest, though of no particular rarity, are mugs and plates produced in anticipation of the Coronation of King Edward VIII (now the Duke of Windsor). Manufacturers are fortunately able to insure themselves against such events not taking place but few could have envisaged in 1936 that the King would abdicate within months of his accession.

Other events in the royal calendar for which pottery souvenirs have been produced include Jubilees: 25th or 50th anniversaries of sovereigns. In this category the earliest examples are pottery mugs celebrating the 50th anniversary of King George III in 1810. Queen Victoria's Golden and Diamond Jubilees (in 1887 and 1897 respectively) were marked by numerous plates, mugs, jugs, vases, busts and figures with inscriptions and verses of patriotic or imperial sentiment. The Silver Jubilee of George V in 1935 inspired souvenir pottery

1937 Coronation souvenirs.
Wedgwood.

on a less lavish scale. Comparatively few examples of commemorative pottery and porcelain have been produced for royal weddings. Deaths in the Royal Family have, surprisingly enough, inspired a number of items, Frederick Prince of Wales (father of George III) and Queen Caroline, the much-maligned wife of George IV, having been mourned in this way.

The investiture of Prince Charles as Prince of Wales at Caernarvon in 1969 produced a spate of mugs, vases, bowls, plates and even money-boxes in a wide variety of materials, ranging from porcelain (Minton) to a new type of ceramic plastic (the Wedgwood Group). A few of these items were manufactured in limited editions but the majority were on unlimited sale.

Saltglaze blue-ground teapot commemorating Frederick the Great c 1760.

In 1954 the British Pottery Manufacturers' Federation presented to the Queen a magnificent bone china vase to commemorate her Coronation. Incorporated at the base of this vase were the ten figures of the Queen's Beasts—the lion, unicorn, red dragon, white horse (Hanover), greyhound (Richmond), yale (Beaufort), falcon (Plantagenet), black bull (Clarence), white lion (Mortimer) and griffin (Edward VII). Subsequently Minton produced replicas of the Beasts in a limited edition and these attractive and unusual souvenirs of

the Coronation are now eagerly sought after by collectors.

It is curious to note that foreign royalty often captured the imagination of the British public and figures of the 'crowned heads' of Europe were favourite subjects for the mid-Victorian Staffordshire flat-backs. A century earlier, however, the exploits of the King of Prussia, Frederick the Great, earned him the admiration of many people in Britain and this was manifest in the jugs, plates and teapots of the 1760s decorated in his honour. Christie's sale of English Pottery and Porcelain

Square bottle portraying
William and Mary.
Dutch-decorated Arita export
ware c 1690.

in October 1969 contained two fine examples of saltglaze teapots embellished with portraits of this king, the coat of arms of Prussia and the motto *"Semper Sublimis'* (Always on top). A Derby jug sold at Sotheby's the following month was inscribed 'Drink Success to the King of Prussia'.

Royal events and personages commemorated in ceramics have not been confined to Britain, though the majority of the examples found in this country are obviously connected with the British Royal Family. Among the items of foreign origin commemorating European royalty sold at Christie's or Sotheby's in recent years have been Copenhagen memorial plaques in honour of the Danish King Frederick VIII and his wife. Of English manufacture but decorated in the Netherlands was a Leeds creamware plate portraying the Stadholder William V and the motto *'Vivat Orange'*. Also of Dutch decoration, though consisting of Japanese export porcelain, was a square bottle portraying William III and Mary. Items such as this were exported from the Arita district by the Dutch East India Company in the seventeenth century.

A charming custom which has recently become established in Britain, though long popular in the Scandinavian countries, is the Christmas plate, a rack-plate with a festive or religious motif produced each year at the Christmas season.

The idea of producing a special plate for Christmas was apparently conceived by the Danish porcelain manufacturers Bing & Grondahl in 1895. Every December since then a plate with an attractive pictorial design has been released in a limited edition. The plates are decorated in underglaze blue and bear the inscription '*Jul Aften*' (Yule-tide) with the date of issue. Winter scenes, snowflakes, Christmas trees, Christmas decorations and customs connected with the Christmas season have been featured on these plates, which are designed by well-known ceramic artists. In addition to the normal-sized annual plates, jubilee plates are produced every five years in a larger format and reproduce the design of one or other of the earlier plates. The jubilee plates made their début in 1915 and, at the time of writing, the most recent was produced in 1970. Similar plates inscribed '*God Jule*' (Good Yule) have been produced by the Royal Copenhagen Porcelain Company since 1908, while other manufacturers in Denmark and Sweden have also issued their series.

In 1969 the idea of Christmas plates was introduced to Britain by Wedgwood, who produced a plate in blue-and-white jasperware. The first of the series showed a view of Windsor Castle and was exquisitely hand-ornamented in white bas-relief with an encircling border of holly leaves and 'Christmas 1969' embossed in blue. This custom was introduced by Wedgwood to celebrate the bicentenary of the establishment of the Wedgwood factory.

The first British Christmas
plate. Wedgwood 1969.

Lowestoft porcelain mug, 1773.

Quite a large amount of pottery has been produced to commemorate personal events, in no way connected with national or international affairs. Under this heading come items recording births, marriages and wedding anniversaries and testimonials to employees for long service.

Probably the best-known items in this field are the large barge teapots which were a speciality of the Midland potters. These enormous teapots, with a miniature teapot set on the lid, frequently richly decorated with floral patterns and inscribed with names and dates, were often intended to commemorate a wedding or a wedding anniversary.

Weddings seem to bring out the worst in some people, judging by the popularity of the so-called bridal chamberpot as a wedding present. These domestic utensils may be found (though very rarely nowadays) with a double-handle—on the same analogy as loving-cups no doubt—and decorated with ribald rhymes. They usually have a frog or frogs crouching on the inside. One unusual variant of this, sold at Christie's in December 1968, however, contained a fine bust of the Duke of Wellington with the caption 'Oh Me, What do I see'.

The more mundane examples of domestic commemorative pottery bear names and dates of people otherwise unknown and were intended as presents to mark christenings or comings of age. Numerous examples of these attractive wares, mugs, plates and tankards, are still available at reasonable cost, although the prices of these are inevitably rising also.

The tremendous increase in interest in pictorial rack-plates in the past few years has encouraged several of the leading manufacturers to produce commemorative pieces of considerable artistic merit. In Britain the leading companies in this field are Wedgwood, Spode, Minton and Doulton, particularly the first two. Among the events which have been commemorated in recent years have been the quatercentenary of William Shakespeare and the death centenary of Charles Dickens. Plates produced by Doulton have portrayed these outstanding literary figures with a surrounding border decorated with vignettes and characters from their writings.

Spode have been commissioned to produce several attractive rack-plates by various bodies. Among the interesting examples of this sort which have appeared in recent years have been the plate marking the golden jubilee of the Royal Air Force and a plate commemorating the 350th anniversary of the Mayflower. The RAF plate, issued in 1968, showed the emblem of the Royal Air Force in the centre, with a border featuring the floral emblems of the United Kingdom and the badges of the Royal Engineers, the Royal Flying Corps and the Royal Naval Air Service, forerunners in the field of military aviation.

The Mayflower plate, commissioned by the Sutton Harbour Improvement Company, appeared early in 1970 to mark the 350th anniversary of the departure of the Pilgrim Fathers from Sutton Harbour, Plymouth. The centre of the plate shows the tiny ship under full sail, while the border is embellished with the emblems of England and America and the civic seals of Plymouth and Plymouth Colony, New England.

Other recent plates from Spode have commemorated the centenary of Girton College and the eighth centenary of the martyrdom of St Thomas à Becket. Many of the Spode productions have an ecclesiastical bias, plates having been issued to commemorate important anniversaries of Westminster, Iona and Selby Abbeys. At the time of writing, another plate to mark the eighth centenary of St Thomas has been commissioned by the Dean and Chapter of Canterbury.

Wedgwood's commemorative wares have ranged from

Modern Spode Iona Abbey plate.

Wedgwood blue-and-white jasper plaque commemorating the first moon landing, 1969.

blue-and-white jasper plaques and plates to earthenware mugs. In the former category the subjects have encompassed such diverse, yet not unrelated, events as the bicentenary of Captain Cook's voyage to the Pacific, and the first moon landing. A simple silhouette portrait of Cook, in the best tradition of blue-and-white jasperware, was used for the former, while the latter, in the same *genre*, showed a bas-relief of the lunar module with the astronauts Neil Armstrong and Edwin Aldrin in the foreground.

Wedgwood, too, have produced Mayflower pieces, and for

Two Wedgwood items commemorating the 350th anniversary of the Mayflower, 1970.

the golden jubilee of the Girl Guide movement they were commissioned by the Girl Guide Association to produce a sweetmeat dish and loving cup in jasperware, and a gaily decorated earthenware mug, all featuring the trefoil motif and a suitable commemorative inscription. A recent rack-plate in creamy white earthenware was issued to mark the centenary of Girton College. An identical version of this plate, but produced in porcelain, was presented to Queen Elizabeth the Queen Mother when she attended the centenary celebrations at Girton in June 1969.

A portrait medallion of
Beethoven, commemorating
the 200th anniversary of
his birth in 1770.
Wedgwood.

During 1970 the Wedgwood group produced a number of commemorative items in various forms and materials. A three-handled loving-cup was produced in blue and white jasper-ware to celebrate the 30th anniversary of the Battle of Britain. The side of this cup was decorated with a Supermarine Spitfire fighter and it is interesting to note that the designer of this famous aircraft, Reginald Mitchell, was himself a native of Stoke-on-Trent, in the heart of the English Potteries. This cup was produced in an edition of 500.

The bicentenary of the birth of Ludwig van Beethoven fell on December 16th 1970 and to mark the occasion Wedgwood produced a black basalt medallion bearing a profile of the composer modelled by Eric Owen. Black basalt, which has been a speciality of Josiah Wedgwood and Sons Ltd since 1769, was the medium employed for a series of portrait busts inaugurated in 1970. The first busts in this series featured General Eisenhower and Abraham Lincoln. Other busts portraying former American presidents, including George Washington, are scheduled for release in future years. Echoing the portrait statuettes of such eminent men of the eighteenth century as Voltaire, Wedgwood have also produced a figure of their founder, Josiah Wedgwood (1730–1795). This statuette, some 8½ inches high, is a black basalt replica of the statue in bronze which stands outside the factory at Barlaston in Staffordshire.

In 1971 the centenary of the opening of the Royal Albert Hall in London was commemorated by a sweet-meat dish in blue and white jasper, with a picture of the concert hall in the centre. The most important anniversary of 1971 was the nineteenth centenary of the city of York (the *Eboracum* of Romano-British times). A limited edition of 1900 Wedgwood bone china plates was commissioned for the occasion. The decoration of this plate includes a finely drawn view of York Minster, with the inscription 'York 71 AD—1971', and this is bordered by a gold inscription in Latin which means 'The history of York is the history of England.' The Rose of York is in gold outline on either side of the view of the Minster and is surrounded by a Roman-style scarlet and gold border. The

Abraham Lincoln. A Black Basalt bust by Wedgwood.

ABRAHAM LINCOLN
President of the United States
1861-1865

A Black Basalt bust of Eisenhower, produced by Wedgwood in a limited edition of 2,000 to introduce a new series commemorating eminent men.

DWIGHT D. EISENHOWER
President of the United States
1953-1961

*One of a limited edition of
100 Coalport Ram's Head
vases in bone china. Made
to commemorate the 1900th
anniversary of the founding
of the City of York.*

rim of the plate shows the York City walls, including the four Bars or gates, and four medallions which depict the arms of the city, the Merchant Adventurers of York, the Merchant Taylors of York and a portrait of the Roman founder, Quintus Petillius Cerealis.

A blue and white jasper sweet dish with the York coat of arms in the centre was also produced in connection with this event. The most expensive item, however, was manufactured in an edition of 100 by the associated company of Coalport and was eagerly snapped up at £100 each. This magnificent Ram's Head vase, based on a style of vessel initiated by Coalport in 1850, bears a hand-painted view of York Minster by Peter Gosling.

In recent years Wedgwood have not only introduced the Christmas plate to Britain (see Chapter 9) but have come up with three ideas of their own. In 1970 this firm began producing an annual calendar plate, the ideal choice for a christening, 21st birthday or silver wedding present. These calendar plates are produced in creamy Queen's Ware with decorative motifs in the border for each of the twelve months.

The custom of remembering mothers during the period of Lent originated in the Middle Ages, when families would gather together and worship in the Mother Church of their area or in the church of their childhood. This was also the occasion to honour the mother of the family with gifts and flowers. During the nineteenth century the custom of Mothering Sunday tended to fade away, but it was revived sixty years ago and, growing in strength through the past two decades, is now an established event in many parts of the world. In 1971 Wedgwood introduced a black basalt Mother's Plate. The charming cameo entitled 'Sportive Love' was designed for Josiah Wedgwood by Lady Elizabeth Templeton and modelled by William Hackwood in 1783.

Wedgwood have not forgotten the children either and in 1971 produced the first Children's Story Plate. The inaugural plate in this series depicted a scene from the story by Hans Christian Andersen entitled '*The Little Sandman*'. This plate was accompanied by a black and white outline of the

CITY OF YORK

illustration for children to colour.

Commemorative mugs are nothing new, this object having long been a favourite for royal events, naval and railway pottery. Impetus to the use of mugs for commemorating persons and events has been given by the Wedgwood group in recent years. Among the subjects represented have been characters from Shakespeare's plays (to mark the quatercentenary of Shakespeare in 1964), Lord Nelson and the Battle of Trafalgar (for the 150th anniversary in 1965), the Chartwell Mug portraying Sir Winston Churchill (1968), characters from operas by Gilbert and Sullivan (1968) and Charles Dickens (to mark the centenary of his death in 1970). These mugs are produced in unlimited editions and have been instrumental in increasing the popularity of commemorative pottery in recent years.

*A Wedgwood Queen's
Ware mug, combining the
head of Churchill and a view
of Chartwell.*

H.P. & W.C. TAYLOR

PERFUMERS

THE BUFFALO HU

One of the most celebrated
of exhibition pot-lids,
The Buffalo Hunt based on
a painting by C. Catlin.

It is ironic to think that although large sums are often expended these days on devising the packaging of merchandise, that packaging is invariably designed for easy destruction or disposal when finished with. This was not the case a century ago, when pride in a product inspired the manufacturer to present it to the consumer in a container which was aesthetically satisfying and worth preserving for its own sake. The best examples of this are the lids of the earthenware jars in which cosmetics and fish pastes were sold in Victorian Britain.

The first of these lids were produced for jars of bear's grease or pomatum used as a hair dressing. Pictures of bears at work or play were common subjects for ornamenting the lids. Similarly jars of fish paste or potted shrimps depicted nautical scenes and views of popular seaside resorts. The vast majority of the pictorial pot-lids were produced by four Staffordshire potteries: Mayer Brothers and Elliott, Ridgeway of Cauldon, Ridgeway of Shelton and F. and R. Pratt of Fenton. Of these, Pratts made the pot-lids which are most esteemed by collectors today.

Pictorial pot-lids might never have arisen above the mundane nature of the goods they enclosed were it not for the Great Exhibition of 1851, at which the pot-lid manufacturers displayed their wares. They broke away from the nautical *genre* on this occasion by producing pot-lids showing the Grand International Building and other views of the Exhibition. In this way the commemorative pot-lid was born.

Pratts produced nine different pot-lids in connection with the Exhibition and featured different views of the Exhibition buildings. There were several variations on these Exhibition pot-lids, with or without an inscription round the edge of the picture, and in various sizes. In some cases two or more versions of the picture exist, differing in minor details. These differences of inscription, size and detail can greatly affect the rarity and value of these pot-lids.

Pratts seem to have had a penchant for exhibitions and a number of later pot-lids were devoted to this subject. Among the events commemorated in this way were the exhibitions held in New York and Dublin in 1853, the International Exhibition of 1862, l'Exposition Universelle held in Paris in 1867, the Philadelphia Centennial Exposition of 1876, the Paris Exhibition of 1878 and the Chicago World's Fair of 1893.

Incidentally the vogue for decorative pot-lids for foodstuffs and cosmetics was beginning to wane by 1870 and had almost completely died out a decade later. Yet some of the finest pictorial pot-lids were produced down to the end of the century. By the 1880's it is obvious that, as their utilitarian purpose was coming to an end, the antiquarian and aesthetic interest of pot-lids was increasing. Quite apart from the pot-lids which were designed as prestige items publicising the great exhibitions of the nineteenth century there were many beautiful lids produced for competitive display at these exhibitions which did not directly refer to the exhibitions. These handsome decorative pieces may be recognised by their broad encircling band of gold and the lavish use of gold in their design.

One of the most celebrated of the exhibition pot-lids in this *genre* is 'The Buffalo Hunt', based on a painting by C. Catlin. At one time this lid held the record price for a single pot-lid, £50 having been paid for it in an auction in 1930. Today a fine example of this celebrated exhibition pot-lid would be worth up to ten times that sum.

Many of the lids produced by Pratts for display at the great nineteenth century exhibitions were commemorative in themselves, bearing historical personages and events. Another highly prized lid is that which depicts General George Washington crossing the Delaware, which Pratts produced especially to mark the Centennial Exposition at Philadelphia in 1876 which celebrated the centenary of the American Declaration of Independence.

A wide variety of pot-lids were produced in the closing years of the last century portraying contemporary personalities (from the Duke of Wellington to Jenny Lind), topical events such as the battles of the Crimean War and reproductions of fashionable paintings of the period. The production of pictorial pot-lids ended abruptly following the death of Jesse Austin, production manager at Pratts, in 1879. Although this

George Washington crossing the Delaware. A pot-lid produced by Pratts to mark the Centennial Exposition at Philadelphia in 1876.

firm ceased to manufacture pot-lids the following year a large quantity of remainders came on the market shortly after Felix Pratt's death in 1894 and it is from that date that the collecting of pot-lids really commenced.

Mounted in circular frames, they make an attractive substitute for miniatures as wall decorations.

Recommended Reading

Bedford, John, *The Collecting Man*, Macdonald, London, 1968.

Fisher, Stanley, *Worcester Porcelain*, Ward Lock, London, 1968.

Godden, Geoffrey A., *British Pottery and Porcelain, 1780-1850*, Arthur Barker, London, 1963.

Godden, Geoffrey A., *Victorian Porcelain*, Herbert Jenkins, London, 1970.

Haggar, Reginald G., *English Pottery Figures 1660-1860*, Tiranti, London, 1947.

Haggar, Reginald G., *English Country Pottery*, Phoenix House, London, 1950.

Haggar, Reginald G., *Staffordshire Chimney Ornaments*, Phoenix House, London, 1955.

Hillier, Bevis, *Pottery and Porcelain 1700-1914*, Weidenfeld & Nicolson, London, 1968.

Imber, Diana, *Collecting Delft*, Arco, London, 1968.

Lane, Arthur, *English Porcelain Figures of the 18th Century*, Faber, London, 1961.

Lewis, Griselda, *A Collector's History of English Pottery*, Studio Vista, London, 1969.

Mackay, James A., *Antiques of the Future*, Studio Vista, London, 1970.

Mankowitz, Wolf, *Wedgwood*, Spring Books, 1966.

Wakefield, Hugh, *Victorian Pottery*, Herbert Jenkins, London, 1962.

Whiter, Leonard, *Spode*, Barrie and Jenkins, London, 1971.